MW00696515

MORE HUMBLE

The Journey Between
Our Flaws, Faith,
and Future

MICHAEL J. HALYARD

©2020 by Michael J. Halyard

All rights reserved. No part of this book may be reproduced in whole or part, or stored in a retrieval system, or transmitted in any form or by any means, electronic, mechanical, photocopying, recording, or otherwise, without the written permission of the author.

ISBN: 978-1-7351176-0-7

Library of Congress Control Number: 2020910204

Printed in Jacksonville, FL, USA by Michael J. Halyard

Disclaimer

The publisher has strived to be as accurate and complete as possible in the creation of this book.

The advice and strategies found within may not be suitable for every situation. This work is sold with the understanding that neither the author nor the publisher is held responsible for the results accrued from the advice in this book.

While all attempts have been made to verify information provided for this publication, the publisher assumes no responsibility for errors, omissions, or contrary interpretation of the subject matter herein. Any perceived slights of specific persons, peoples, or organizations are unintended.

For bulk book orders, contact Michael J. Halyard by emailing Halyardministries@gmail.com.

Dedication

This piece of art is dedicated to humanity. It is not only for preacher's kids, chaplains, and spiritual caregivers. It applies to (but is and not limited to) nurses, administrative clerks, barbers, beauticians, teachers, realtors, athletes, entrepreneurs, CNAs, social workers, clergy, business owners, and judicial and political professionals. From the richest to the poorest. I don't care if you're on the end of a stethoscope or a broomstick, the judge's bench or behind bars, saved and sanctified or engulfed with illegal substances.

Being "More Humble" is a practice of humility that each and every one of us can be an active participant. As we live in a world where some appear to live a lifestyle of entitlement, the reality is, if it was not for the grace of God on our sides, where would we all be...?

This is dedicated to those who are willing to go beyond "the norm," wanting to overcome the odds and traditions, and stretch towards something greater than themselves for the sake of a higher purpose, regardless of the hand life has dealt them. The single parenting mother or father who's wondered why they have had to raise their children alone; the divorced man or woman who at night feels the angst of being let up to be let down. The follower of the Divine whose life doesn't "look squeaky clean and polished." This is dedicated to those who struggle, who hurt, cry, have had successes, but also disappointments. Those who've graduated but also failed. Those who are free externally but feel as if they are in bondage internally at times.

This is dedicated to those who have sacrificed for the sake of their calling and the vision the Divine has placed uniquely upon your life.

There is no secret what God can do. What He's done for others, He'll do for you!

Table of Contents

Introduction

*"The problem with 'being strong'
is that nobody expects you to ever have
a weak moment."*

MH

Have you experienced:

Dreams - The desire to be the best you can be?

Success/Failures - Having been let up to be let down?

Hopes - The desire for a new day, but at times...

Life - Seems like just a mirage...

I can resonate with you. My journey to being "More Humble" began as I sought to self-reflect and ask myself the question, "How are you doing?" So in turn, I ask you...

How are you **really** doing today? A question that I've consistently asked myself throughout the course of my lamentable yet fortunate life. In this book, I share how I have come to find meaning and purpose through my flaws and faith. My journey to being "More Humble" has allowed me to play to my strengths and train to my weaknesses.

In the midst of being "a preacher's kid," chaplain, and spiritual leader of humanity, it is my prayer and hope that my brokenness helps you more than my "put-togetherness" ever did. Through my story in this book, you will discover that your greatness lies within your difference. Therefore, it is the sum of the parts that equates to a greater outcome.

Writing a book has always been a dream, but this reality as you are reading has been a new adventure and journey for me. I'm reminded of when I entered Clinical Pastoral Education (CPE) Training for the first time. I didn't know what to expect but I was willing to trust the process. I can recall an individual telling me, "Michael, don't be a cowboy!" We tend to use this expression in the military a lot, but a Cowboy in this context could also be a term used to describe someone who was wild; given to act impulsively. It is my knowledge that originally, a cowboy was an individual who tended cattle (Beef Stock). They had to be an expert in the saddle and an expert with a rope. In chaplaincy, I quickly found out that I could not be the expert of converting and pushing my own (agenda) spiritual saddle of righteousness onto someone. If anything, this mindset got me bucked off my "high horse" several times.

In this book, you will find various practical principles and applications of *humbling* experiences such as this. As a chaplain, my calling to the ministry has provided me Divine opportunities to enter into sacred spaces where people are happy, celebratory, and sometimes emotional, but also hurting, distraught, and tearful. This is humbling because I too have been there and even today, often have experiences as such. Through Clinical Pastoral Education (CPE) I have learned not to shy away from the pain of my past, but to embrace its teachings. As God used the campus chaplain Ray Penn in undergraduate school to listen empathically, I understand that offering God's presence and my support is better than some words. I have come to realize that we are the hands in which God chooses to do His work, His legs to help carry others, and the presence He uses to show Himself. I believe it is through our emptiness God's presence is seen. I now continue to grow and understand that compassion, love, and most of the time silence also reveals the presence of God. My patience with God's timing and my tendency to take on a lot are still growth edges that I continuously work on. My past has not been perfect, but the experience it has provided me makes perfect sense as it has made me who I am. For that reason, I embrace it in order to learn more about myself and others.

Almighty God: Today, confirm my calling, affirm my assignment, deflate my ego, develop my discernment, open my eyes, heal my heart, evaluate my relationships, and allow your will to be done.

Amen

Chapter 1

10 – 2 – 82

"You've never seen a butterfly hang out with caterpillars… It's ok to outgrow people."

MH

And there we are. Mom, (the twins) Kenneth, Kevin, Monique, and myself. I am a 37-year-old African American male, born and raised in Jacksonville, Florida. Being raised by a Baptist Pastor, these have been my denominational roots since birth. My father, Morris J. Halyard, was born in St. Augustine, Florida and was raised by his grandmother as his parents were at a very young age upon conceiving.

My mother, Patricia A. Robinson, was born and raised in Jacksonville, Florida. They met within a period of their life when they were both staying in the Blodgett homes (*low income housing*) at the time. My father worked various odd jobs as he was trying to provide for a family, go to college to better himself, and as I was born, serve as a pastor of a church. My mother worked at Popeye's Chicken for a great length of time but also worked as a home health aide.

She was encouraged by my father to go back to school, which she did. My mother went back to junior college and obtained her culinary arts certificate and then managed the church's restaurant until she could no longer do so. My mother is now disabled and has numerous health complications from COPD, a disk rupture in her back, and sleep apnea, to name a few.

My father was once a school teacher at Northwestern Middle School. He also served in the military and worked as both an employee of the city of Jacksonville and the Duval Medical Examiner's Office. He finally retired from the Medical Examiner's Office and as a U.S. Army Officer.

My parents have raised a number of children, but we do not all have the same biological father and mother. There are eleven of us total (*that we know of...* LOL); nine boys and two girls. My sister Monique and I are the closest of all my brothers and sisters, mainly because we had more interaction growing up than my other siblings. Before she moved out, Monique and I lived with my mother.

My parents never got married. I would always wonder why I could not have the same type of family I'd seen on The Cosby Show? Why couldn't everything be "normal?" As I was growing up as the youngest (*on my mother's side*), my siblings had moved out, had established families of their own, or were either off in the military, jail, prison, or on their own course of life.

I saw very little of them at a young age, but learned a lot from them, particularly, some choices and decisions made of what **not** to do. Most of my brothers not only sold drugs but were on drugs (*cocaine and marijuana*), which took their lives on a downward spiral. Of the eleven of us, nine have been incarcerated.

Growing up, my family and I have been down some dark roads of poverty, crime, drugs, and debt, which stained my mind early on to believe that life would not get any better.

Michael (top left) in elementary school at the time when so much was changing

Nevertheless, this has helped shape me into the person I am today.

Despite my family dynamics, I am humbled by the presence of redemption, grace, and mercy. You see, that's what it has taken for me to be the me I am today. The pain, struggle, and disappointments have not been in vain.

Dear God: Today, don't let me hold on to what you've released. Strengthen me to birth what you've conceived and empower me to finish what I've started.

Amen

*Siblings, Monique, Kenneth, Kevin, and
Michael, experiencing a moment of hope*

Chapter 2

THE BEST I CAN

"Your greatness is in your difference."

MH

Growing up, I had a passion and zeal for sports. I would watch highlights from various sporting events and would convince myself that one day, I too would hit a home-run, catch the game-winning touchdown, or make a game-winning shot. Truthfully, I just wanted to be the best I could be. I felt as if this was a way out from the ordinary day-to-day of spending too much time around the house or having to go to church. After school and once homework was completed, chores were done, and depending on my conduct for the day, I was granted permission to go outside and play with my neighborhood friends. We would all walk or ride our bikes to the neighborhood park and play either baseball, football, or basketball all evening long. However, I had to be back home before the streetlights came on.

If not, there would be a belt waiting for me at the front door. Or even worse, I would more than likely get embarrassed in front of everyone. I received many spankings and beatings from my parents growing up. They would tell me that "this is going to hurt me more than it hurts you." I would often find myself baffled by the mitigated gale of such a remark, but later on in life, I have come to understand the meaning associated with the pain. My parents did not believe in time-out. Rather, they believed your time would be out the moment you failed to adhere to the rules and regulations they had disseminated.

You see, being the best you can be is challenging. You have to be honest enough to say, 'yes, I am good and moving in the right direction.' Then you also have to be able to pull back, reflect and say 'yes, I have some areas of growth.' Perfection is not the goal. However, progress is!

I strongly believe this is what my parents were attempting to teach me in a way that might be a little different than other cultures. My brothers and sisters, I have come to discover that *"Your greatness is in your difference"* … not in who we idolize, try and imitate, and pattern our lifestyles after. It is not in our following on "the Gram," Twitter, or Facebook. It's in the complexity and simplicity of your humanity. The Bible declares in Psalm 139:14, "I praise you, for I am fearfully and wonderfully made. Wonderful are your works; my soul knows it very well."

In the picture, you'll witness Monique holding me. Discipline has a unique way of holding us not only accountable, but up to a standard of humbleness. Who is it that's able to hold you and love you, yet allow you to be the best you can be? Who is it that sees the difference in your uniqueness and holds on to you in spite of your imperfections?

*Monique holding Michael at home in front of
her Honda Civic; we loved that car*

One of the reasons I loved Monique's little red Honda Civic was because this was the vehicle Dad allowed us to shift the gears while he steered and operated the gas, clutch, and brakes. I have discovered that being the best you can be requires that you be able to trust the process – shift gears while the DIVINE (*takes the wheel*) steers and allows you to move forward (*gas*) or slows you down (*brakes*) when you do not have enough sense to do it yourself.

My close relationship with my sister has developed over time through the concept of the vehicle. It has been through times where we have needed each other to hold one another up when we have felt like (*crashing*) giving up. As long as I can remember, she has always tried to support me in athletics, encouraged me through my dreams, and even in the midst of my failures in life, has helped me explore that my greatness has been within my difference. Through our relationship, I am reminded of how my mind was shaped by the areas of my life that traverse my environment.

This song was written in 2019. I debuted it at an all-staff retreat for Veterans Healthcare System Of the Ozarks - VHSO.

The Best I Can:

I just want to be the best I can…
It's hard to understand
Sometimes I want to go
But I know there is more

The road seems so long
As I drive I feel alone
That's why…I need you in my life
That's why…we need you in our life

I don't want to go
But I know
The road of life, can be so tough
Sometimes I feel from day to day
What I hold inside, I need to say
Forget my flaws and all mistakes

I just want to be the best I can…
It's hard to understand
Sometimes I want to go
But I know there is more

The road seems so long
As I drive I feel alone
That's why...I need you in my life
That's why...we need you in our life

Monique and Michael after church one day

Chapter 3

THE PREACHER'S KID "PK"

"As long as God is pleased, it doesn't matter who isn't."

MH

I attended Jean Ribault Middle School (1995 - 1997) in Jacksonville, Florida. As I was continuously active in sports, I began to explore other elements of life as well. I begin to gain more self-confidence during this period of my life. My social skills were beginning to expand as I was welcomed by many around campus. Most of my friends I knew from growing up in the same neighborhood, and there were some I met just by eating lunch in the cafeteria or hanging around other people.

There were many times a group of us would plan to hang out together, and then, I'd have to give the usual response, "I have to go to church." It seemed like everyone else was having fun and enjoying life, while mine was consumed by church. For a long time, my parents never came to any of my games to support me. My sister Monique would be there or a member of the church whose son played on the same team with me.

From time to time, I'd wonder what it would feel like not to go to church today? However, the rules of the house were that "as long as you stay under this roof, you're going to church." I would always say to myself, "I can't wait until I grow up so I can choose whether or not I want to go to church." I felt as if the church was more important to my parents than family. My father was very stern and strict, and my mother would support him in his decisions. It had felt as if they had married the church but divorced our family. Speaking of family, I think that I'll introduce you to my siblings throughout this chapter.

Once, another family was almost created. During this period of time, I found someone who I truly cared about, a young lady by the name of T-Dub. We dated for an extended period of time. T-Dub became pregnant during the course of the time we dated but had a miscarriage. I was very nervous, afraid, and at a loss of what to say or do when she told me initially that she was pregnant. I just knew my parents would have some choice words for me if they didn't kill me first!

We would have been a very young couple trying to raise a child, but I guess it was not meant to be. Shortly after, we tried to continue our relationship, but she had found someone else. At the time, she enjoyed dating older men. I believe she ended up having a relationship with her child's father. This hurt me greatly, but I did have the opportunity to mentor and groom her son as best as I knew how to. I am grateful for that. No matter who I have dated that have had children, I have always tried to support, encourage, motivate, and be an example of what a father can be.

In June of 2001, I graduated from Jean Ribault Senior High School (1998-2001).

I continuously remained active in sports. I played football, basketball, and ran track and field. As a ninth grader, I was amazed by the juniors and seniors. They looked different, sounded different, and acted different. It seemed as if some of them didn't have anyone making them go to church, Sunday school, choir rehearsal, or vacation Bible school. I thought that was pretty cool. I wanted to fit in and be like them. I began to drink alcohol and smoke marijuana from time to time. By the tenth grade, my father had bought me a white 1991 Ford Crown Victoria from the local car auction. He was the best dad in the world for making this purchase. Now I had somewhat of a means of freedom.

Growing up, I dreaded the reality of going to church and having to pretend that everything was ok. Everything should be ok, right? Surely the pastor and his family were "holy." This was the pressure and unwelcome expectations from people that I felt every time we entered the doors of the church or were seen in public. Since my father was "a pastor," we should not be doing anything wrong. We had to have it all together.

Needless to say, by the time I was born, my father had stopped smoking and his drinking started slowly decreasing as well. However, I did not know what alcohol was until I found myself browsing around the house as children do and finding a bottle of Bourbon and a six-pack of beer. I did not know about vulgarity until I experienced it first-hand in my own household. By then, two of my brothers were incarcerated as well. It struck me as odd how we were supposed to be the family that had it all together, but in actuality everything was really falling apart before my eyes.

At various times growing up, I recall my mother being tearful and distraught because she did not understand why my father would never marry her. So in high school, I found myself clinging to those who patterned the life I lived with for so long. If my parents had liquor and beer, why couldn't I? If my father once smoked, why couldn't I? If my parents never dreamed about getting married one day, why should I?

Although I am venting in my lament, this is how I'd rationalized in my mind doing what I wanted to do. My brothers and sisters, there's a lot of things you can't control in life. You can't control who your parents are, or the dynamics that are associated within the context of your family.

Nevertheless, there are two things you can control in life and that is your *attitude and effort*! You may ask, "Michael, how do you implement this control?" It is my experience that this process has to be a persistent endeavor in doing something that is difficult. In life there is a lot that comes to you from different directions, as you seek to maintain your sanity. As we understand that we possess the ability to identify and change certain aspects of our lives, we can significantly influence our future. This knowledge can drive your attitude and effort towards positive change. When we are hit with adversity, it doesn't take much effort to quit. If your self-belief isn't strong enough, you won't subdue the obstacles. Instead, you may find yourself subject to sabotaging that which could be.

When it comes down to the nitty-gritty of things, I am a "PK." Good, bad, ugly, or indifferent, I am the son of a preacher man and proud of it. My siblings I love and will always appreciate.

Almighty God: Today, hide me in your hand, keep my eyes on the prize, let nothing hang over my head, don't let me take grace for granted, forgive me for falling short, and give me courage where I am vulnerable.

Amen

*The Reverend Doctor Morris J. Halyard (Dad)
and Michael J. Halyard*

Michael's brothers "Chucky and Mickey"

Michael's brothers, Kenneth and Kevin, and his Dad after church on Father's Day

Michael's sister "Adrian"

*Michael's sister Monique and
"Skinny Morris"*

*Michael's brother Cedric, sister Monique,
and brother Morris III "Moe"*

More pictures of Michael's siblings: Monique, Chucky, Cedric, Kenneth, Morris III, Morris (COL), Mickey, Kevin, Big Boy

Chapter 4

LET UP TO BE LET DOWN

*"Sometimes the promise is linked
to the pain."*

MH

It's easy to dismiss Judas as a villain or a victim, but I'm struck by the fact that, in many ways, I was just like him. Judas was a follower of Jesus and a preacher of the gospel, but there was a capriciousness about him. In the end, he abandoned the faith he once professed.

When I felt that I was betrayed, I had turned away from faith. I could care less. However, I had to remind myself how Christ might've felt when those whom he cared about and loved so dearly did not want anything to do with him for whatever reason. If they did Christ that way, why would I feel that I am any different? - *More Humble*.

Have you ever been let up to be let down? What a horrible feeling. I've been engaged twice in my life. The shame and embarrassment that it has caused still leaves a bitter taste in my mouth at times. Relationships take work. It is not easy! In today's society it seems as if when people meet at the altar and announce the words, "I do," it really seems to translate into the definition of "I'll try."

My brothers and sisters, I believe we all desire to have someone in our corner whom we can confide in and love unconditionally even if and when they get on our nerves. My humble experience within the let downs of my past relationships have led me to believe that just because you're married or in a relationship, does not mean that you have mastered the art of the marriage/relationship. It requires time and experience to fulfill your title.

I cannot fault or point the finger at anyone else. At the end of the day, people have the freewill of choice. We may not always agree with their choices. Nevertheless, we all have the right to choose how we handle the situation. I remember when I was a first year Clinical Pastoral Education (CPE) Resident, and during my individual supervision (IS), I asked my supervisor, "How do I know when I have found 'the right one?'" His response was simple and made sense. In a calming, moderate voice, he softly asked me, "When you go into the shoe store, do you buy the first pair that you see…?" Wow...

Listen, everyone is not made for you. Not everyone can handle the anointing that's upon your life. There's nothing wrong with you and there is nothing wrong with them. It's a matter of choice to be selective, not desperate.

I was at Burger King the other day. I had just finished my Whopper and I was down to the last of my Sprite. I found myself slurping, continuously attempting to drink out of the straw when there was not much left. Then it hit me. Throw away the straw. You don't have to act thirsty when He promised that your cup would overflow (Psalm 23:5).

A word of encouragement here: Never pretend to be someone else just so you can be with someone else. At the end of the day, if it costs you your peace, it's too expensive and you can't afford it.

My brothers and sisters, it's a new day!

Almighty God: Today, enrich those who are feeling poor in spirit, enlarge those who feel trapped in a tight situation, and empower those weakened by draining relationships.

Amen

Chapter 5

A New Day

"If you're looking for flaws, use a mirror not a telescope."

MH

Often people show you their stars and their trophies, but never reveal their battles and scars. My conversion experience was a battle (*internally*) in itself. However, it has become the springboard of my success.

Upon my return from college, things had turned around in my life. However, there was still a void and an emptiness that I was feeling, and I couldn't put my fingers on just what it was. I felt as if I was doing everything "right," but I had failed to realize although I was doing what was "right," I wasn't doing what I was called to do.

I received my calling to the ministry in 2007, after an array of life-altering events. I had several failed relationships, encounters with the law, and indulged in heavy alcohol use, while at the same time, still searching for who I was. I still continued to defer from acknowledging and accepting my calling from the Lord. In the latter years of undergraduate school, I found myself taking philosophy and religion classes, attending worship services regularly, and taking on the campus chaplain (*Father Ray Penn*) as my mentor. I had a sense of what ministry was about growing up in the church and watching my father as pastor, but being the pastor of a traditional church myself had never been a God-given or driven affirmation within my calling.

During the fall of 2007, I was at a church in St. Augustine, Florida and I was convicted by the Holy Spirit then to yield and submit unto the calling that the Lord had placed upon my life. No longer could I run, hide, or deny the fact that I had been called by the Lord for ministry. As shocking as it was to me initially, it was confirming to others. Throughout my life, it was often told to me from others that they had seen the presence of the Lord upon my life and they felt that I had a calling on my life at an early age.

It was later confirmed by my parents that they had set me aside and dedicated me to the Lord at a young age in which they asked God to use me for the intended purpose of His ministry.

I was licensed on January 8, 2008 and on October 9, 2011 I was ordained. As I embraced the calling on my life to the ministry, I wasn't sure if it would be within the perimeters of the pastorate, or of a multi-faith, multicultural, chaplain perspective. I grew up in a Baptist church as a pastor's son, in a predominately African-American neighborhood, educational system, and social environment.

However, when I went off to college, it was a new day for me. I was able to experience a variety of faiths and cultures that were different from my traditional Baptist beliefs.

*Michael in St. Louis getting ready to see
Lenny Kravitz live in concert*

I felt the call of God upon my life and a spiritual interest in wanting to explore and minister to the world from the perspective of others. However, with holding on to my own values and beliefs, chaplaincy continues to grant me the liberty and freedom to make room for a non-judgmental pastoral presence with others.

Dear God: Stretch my thinking, extend my reach, enlarge my circle, enrich my experiences, and maximize my potential.
                                                        Amen

Chapter 6

MIRAGE

"When you don't have focus, distractions look like opportunities."

MH

This song was written in 2019 after waking up from a dream. I debuted it in 2020 at my book release at the Fayetteville Town Center – Fayetteville, AR.

Is it all a Mirage I see?
Are you there waiting for me?

When I look into your eyes
I'm filled with hope and still mesmerized

To a place that I just want to be
Where the sky is blue
And we're so free

Your warm embrace
Your smiling face
Is where I want to be.

Is it all a Mirage I see?
I feel so lost... where should we be

The mutual feelings seem the same
The isle is clear we just need a ring

To a place that I just want to be
Where the sand is white
With the ocean breeze

I want it so…
Can't let you go…
Is where I want to be.

Have you found what you're looking for out of life? Better yet, what in particular are you looking for in life, or is it all a mirage you see? Maybe you are discouraged because your

past seems to haunt your present potential. Maybe you feel that you are not qualified. The devil would have us believe these things are true, but he is a liar!

I'm reminded of a story about a little girl who proudly wore a shiny cross on a chain around her neck. One day her preacher noticed how proud she seemed to be of her pretty cross, and said to her, "Honey, don't you know that the cross Jesus died on wasn't beautiful like the one you're wearing? It was an ugly, terrible, wooden thing."

The little girl smiled and replied: "Oh, I know that. But they told me in Sunday school that whatever Jesus touches, He changes."

Dear God: Today, allow me to fall in love with life again, force me to break up with who I used to be, marry me to my destiny, and put a restraining order on my fears.

Amen

Chapter 7

Go Wash Your Hands

"Once you carry your own water, you learn the value of every drop."

MH

Never in my life would I have thought that something so pandemic as the COVID-19 (Coronavirus) would take place. However, this chapter was well-thought-out prior to the virus going viral. While surfing the internet one day I couldn't help but notice the World Health Organization - Public Service Announcement, "Do The Five." Of those five topics, washing your hands was #1.

DO THE FIVE

Help stop coronavirus

1. HANDS Wash them often
2. ELBOW Cough into it
3. FACE Don't touch it
4. SPACE Keep safe distance
5. HOME Stay if you can

You would think it'd be a no brainer to wash our hands regularly given the various toxic areas they come across on a day-to-day basis. However, washing your hands with soap and water or using an alcohol-based hand sanitizer kills viruses that may be on your hands.

Too often in life, we as individuals continue to carry viruses that have weakened our spiritual immune systems. Often, when we wash our hands we immediately touch the very element that is toxic and dirty again (the faucet handle). Instead of first reaching for the paper towel (safety) and using that element (tool) to turn off the faucet, we expose ourselves to the very toxin that we were hoping to wash away.

Michael, having a moment of clarity

My brothers and sisters, how many times have we "washed away" people that were abusive (mental/ emotional/ physical), did not have our best interest at heart, or could flat out just not give a damn about our personal well-being but yet we "cared" about them?

Sure, we can practice "social distancing," but what happens when your heart is still very much connected? We should respond to crises with a faithful preparedness, not a fearful panic.

As we have all come together during such a time of COVID-19, it is my prayer that our sacrifice and love for humanity doesn't stop when it is over.

Could it be that some people are brought into our lives for a season and not to remain permanently? The reasoning behind this may never be known. At the end of the day, you cannot force anyone to see your value. It was *Maya Angelou* who said, "Love recognizes no barriers. It jumps hurdles, leaps fences, penetrates walls to arrive at its destination full of hope." Therefore, don't be too upset when you are stabbed in the back. More than likely they were aiming for your heart. So go wash your hands. Remember, some things in life you learn more from experience than you do instruction.

Spirit of the living God: **DEHYDRATE** *my doubts,* **NOURISH** *my ideas,* **FEED** *my dreams,* **STARVE** *my insecurities, and prepare a* **TABLE** *in front of my enemies.*

Amen

Chapter 8

Black Man – White House

"The highest form of ignorance is rejecting knowledge from an area you know nothing about."

MH

Many may not be familiar with what I'm looking at in the picture on the left. Neither would I have known the splendor that is germane with humility. It wasn't until this black man was invited to the White House.

But Michael, how did you get there? The more I continue to mature in my faith, the more I attempt to make my prayers less personal: and more, "Lord, let your will be done." I asked the Lord to place me in the position He would have me in so I could reach the world. He granted me that opportunity.

However, let me interject that this has not simply come through osmosis! I have taken unwanted assignments, made sacrifices, burned the midnight oil, studied, poured into the ministry God has called me to, and have picked up and moved in my ministry through faith. What this created was Divine exposure which touched the hearts of others to invite me to our nation's Capitol to pray. It was nothing that I had said or done that was so great. What this humbling experience shows you is the omnipotent power of God. In the words of **The Williams Brothers** – *"I'm just a nobody, trying to tell everybody, about Somebody, who saved my soul."*

However, a lot of people want the glory, but they are not interested in the sacrifice associated with success. While there are some on social media trying to be popular by likes and views, they compromise to get recognized. My brothers and sisters, if you're not in the room where changes are occurring, you're stuck in the yard where consequences are received. As a Nation, I believe we have made great strides in pivoting from slavery to equal opportunity.

Slavery existed in many cultures, dating back to early human civilizations. A person could become enslaved from the time of their birth, capture, or purchase. On September 22, 1862, President Abraham Lincoln issued the preliminary Emancipation Proclamation, which declared that as of January 1, 1863, all slaves in the states currently engaged in rebellion against the Union "shall be then, thenceforward, and forever free."

As an African-American male, with an African-American father (*born in 1942*), I am proud to state that racism was never tolerated, taught, or encouraged! Yet, it became a tool my parents and family used in order to help me treat all as brothers and sisters in Christ.

After graduating from high school, I attempted to go to a HBCU (Historical Black Colleges and Universities). This was sort of the "norm" for African-Americans who grew up in my part of town. Needless to say, the Historical Black Colleges and Universities (HBCUs) that I applied to either did not accept me or respond to my

request. I wondered what the reasoning was behind the disappointment at the time. Years later, I now sense the humbling experience of what God was trying to show me.

> *#1 Not everything you want is what you really need.*
>
> *#2 Just because things don't happen when you want it to, doesn't mean that it never will.*

As I was settling for my comfort zone culturally (*people who looked and displayed the same type of behaviors as I did*), God was opening my eyes and stretching me for His intended purpose to the call of a worldwide ministry. He was preparing me for something bigger (Chaplaincy). In doing so, I have had so much help on my journey.

Oh by the way, guess what school I graduated from and received my BA Degree in Communication Arts? Abraham Lincoln's School (LMU), Lincoln Memorial University Harrogate, Tennessee. When no one else would at the time, Lincoln Memorial University (LMU) gave me an opportunity. They looked beyond my grades, lack of grade point average, and took a chance on an average, young black boy from Jacksonville, Florida.

I believe Lincoln personally hated slavery and considered it immoral. He once stated, "If the negro is a man, why then my ancient faith teaches me that `all men are created equal;' and that there can be no moral right in connection with one man's making a slave of another." He said this in a now-famous speech in Peoria, Illinois, in 1854.

Michael next to the statue of
Abraham Lincoln

I would not be where I am today on my own. It has taken those: *past, present, and future,* such as Lincoln, Dr. Martin Luther King Jr., Blacks, Whites, Christians, Non-Christians, people of all cultures, races, faiths, and sociological kinesics that have impacted my life. I am able to have the means of freedom by sacrifices from those, who long before my time paved the way for myself and others. There are those who have been treated immorally, gunned down with their hands up in a posture of surrender, beaten, spit upon and tortured in hopes of one day a black man could enter the White House, be able to walk inside, pray over our Nation, and experience being able to *look towards the hills from whence cometh my help. My help cometh from the Lord, which made heaven and earth.* **Psalm 121:1-2**.

I have sense enough to believe that not everyone who shares your color isn't always your kind and everyone who is your kind isn't always of the same color. I hope that makes sense. My brothers and sisters, *love goes beyond the barriers* (LGBTB). Does racism still exist? You better believe it does!

Congressman John Rutherford (FL), House of Representatives Speaker Paul Ryan, CH (CPT) Michael Halyard, and Father Patrick Conroy

However, I am encouraged by the passage of scripture that denotes: *Thou preparest a table before me in the presence of mine enemies: thou anointest my head with oil; my cup runneth over.* **Psalm 23:5**. You see, if there are no enemies then the testimony that lies within the table can't be prepared. Therefore, I thank God for the haters, nay-sayers, doubters, and those who choose to dislike me because of the color of my skin or any other reason. This allows me to experience the Glory of God even more. When you know that others do not want to see you succeed and God allows you to anyway, that should make us all the more grateful, thankful, and humble. Therefore, respond with success and *achievement in every field of human endeavor* instead of reacting out of anger and resentment. In times such as this, America, we need unity and not division. As we face fluctuating economics, threats from abroad, unrest at home, or other troubling circumstances, God is not caught unaware. For He is the one who gave us this promise in **2 Chronicles 7:14:** *"If my people, who are called by My name, will humble themselves and pray and seek my face and turn from their wicked ways, then I will hear from heaven and will forgive their sin and will heal their land."*

WELCOMING CHAPLAIN MICHAEL J. HALYARD;
Congressional Record Vol. 163, No. 181
(House of Representatives - November 07, 2017)

Merciful and loving God, source of life and constant guide to Your people, we ask Your blessings on our esteemed representatives as they continue to help govern a course for our nation and its citizens.

In these days of disrepute and impropriety, keep them steadfast in their deliberations. Inspire them to continue in their journey to promote the values upon which this great Nation was founded: justice, liberty, equality, freedom, and peace.

As Your blessings of goodness transcend into a dynamic of creativity, help us to see signs of hope born of pain as we often find ourselves present in the midst of uncertainty and suffering.

May the vacuous space left by stains of catastrophic occurrences open the minds and hearts of all to deeper compassion and a new level of human understanding.

May all that is done here today be for our American democracy while reflecting Your resplendent honor and glory. Amen.

Almighty God: Give me patience for the process, give me grace for the journey, and tolerance for the intolerable.

Amen

Chapter 9

RIDE OR DIE?

"Support is a verb..."

MH

Doug in the beginning phase of helping me build Bentley's feeder

Everything that matters in life has to be built. My friend Doug and I started a project that I had envisioned for my baby boy – Bentley.

Pieces of wood and tools used to build the feeder

Although I possessed the idea, I did not have the tools to build that which I desired and envisioned. You see, the building materials, tools, equipment, and building practices you implement will make or break the success of your project.

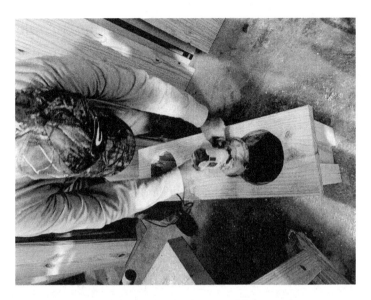

Doug sanding down the wood

As you notice within the pictures, there is *a process* that builds up to the end goal. I am no expert in this area at all, but I believe that when general contractors or subcontractors sign on to construction projects, they usually start off believing everything will run smoothly. However, during the course of the work, issues sometimes arise that force all parties to go their separate ways. If the contractor does not show up, it could be considered "abandonment."

I honestly have not dated many people in my life. Romantic relationships have not withstood the build in my life. I believe it's because when the saw-dust begins to build up and the labor that's needed to sustain the vision is tested, it has been easier for others to walk away and abandon the job, rather than to finish it.

The foundation had been built and set

The process continues

The actual end product

I could not have built the dog feeder alone. It took me knowing my limitations, but also embracing my strengths. Who is it that is helping you build something greater out of your life? Are they with you because it's *official* or simply because it's *beneficial*?

Michael and Bentley in our Adidas and Adidog Outfits

Although he can walk, sometimes you need someone to pick you up. As I'm holding him, I am reminded how much he has picked me up. Therefore, what appears to be big and heavy, my fur-baby has helped me carry the very things that used to carry me.

Dear God: Help me let go of what I've lost, allow me to celebrate what I have left, and push me to focus on where you are leading me.

Amen

Chapter 10

A Sporty Spirit

*"If you have a dream or goal that you can
achieve on your own, chances are
it's too small."*

MH

I have made mention earlier that sports have always been near and dear to my heart. I am a New York Yankees, Dallas Cowboys, Florida Gators, and Los Angeles Lakers fan. It is so captivating that, no matter the weather, location, or obstacles that occur, my teams tend to excel. Now, most of you Eagles, FSU, or Celtics fans may not agree, but that's ok (LOL).

Seriously though, maybe this will grab your attention. For me, I believe that there is a spirit that coincides with sports or what I perceive as having a sporty spirit. This, my friends, becomes the celebration of the human mind, body, and spirit (*whole health*), and is reflected in values we find in and through sports. Just like others around the globe, I too miss watching sports live or on television. As we have hit a season without sports during this (COVID-19) pandemic, I feel that the absence of sports has helped me to appreciate the principles correlated within sports. This is to include but not limited to: Ethics, fair-play and honesty; health; excellence in performance; character and education; fun and joy; teamwork; dedication and commitment; respect for rules and laws; respect for self and other participants; courage; community, and solidarity.

From my faith tradition, my Lord and Savior had a sporty spirit. He too had a team. The Twelve Disciples: (Not in any particular order).

Peter: Bold, emotional, over talker, type "A" leader who was willing to risk it all. He had to learn to listen to others and submit to Christ.

John: Brilliant, calculated, a leader who loved justice. He became unstoppable when he fully accepted the work of Christ. This acceptance of Christ's justice led this "son of thunder" to become the Apostle of love.

Matthew: The tax collector, the traitor to his people whom Jesus named "the gift of God." One of the greatest conversion stories in the New Testament and a lesson that no one is too lost to turn to Jesus and become a central part of his mission.

Thomas: A natural doubter and pessimist who became a powerful missionary when he chose Jesus and stuck to it.

Philip: The Hellenist, a Jew who grew up looking like a Greek. Philip probably would have looked, acted, and talked like an outsider to the Jews. His strength was his ability to connect with people; his weakness was a propensity to look too much like the culture.

Simon: The one who was associated with a group of politically and at times militantly motivated Jews who vehemently opposed Greek culture and specifically Roman rule.

Only Jesus could combine a team with Philip the Hellenist (adopted Greek culture), Matthew the tax collector, and Simon the Zealot into one group and unify them.

My brothers and sisters, I strongly believe that only an eternal mission/goal/championship will break through our earthly preferences.

Michael at the new Yankee Stadium

Judas: Unlike Paul, Judas was in the right crowd, heard the correct teachings, and followed the right leader, yet his heart was off. He loved money more than Jesus. He followed Jesus because it was a smart fiscal decision. This heart would lead him to turn his back on his team and take his own life.

Andrew: Brother of Peter, fisherman, originally a disciple of John the Baptist. (Mark 1:16-18)

Bartholomew: His name means "Son of Tolmai." Some believe he may have been from royal blood. Tradition teaches that he was a scholar and a searcher of Scripture. Many believe Bartholomew was an evangelistic partner of Philip and Thomas and suffered martyrdom in Armenia.

James the Elder: Brother of John and a fisherman.

James the Lesser: The phrase "lesser" probably means younger. Tradition teaches he was crucified in Egypt for his faith and worked as a missionary.

Jude, **Thaddeus**, or **Lebbeus:** Often called the man with three names. He was also a Zealot like Simon.

Michael at his first ever Red Sox vs Yankees game

I believe that it is through having a sporty spirit there are guiding values that if properly adhered to, can put us in the position of winning. I mean, really...be honest, who likes losing? However, when we do lose, it doesn't mean we have failed in life. Matter of fact, the hope for redemption and avoiding a *losing streak* is found inside of what I consider the *playbook* for our lives. The Holy Bible.

Hopefully, you can clearly see that there were 12 different individuals. This meant 12 different personalities, ways of thinking, behaviors, but they eventually had one common purpose.

Michael at the Red Sox vs Yankees game

*Michael at his first Chicago Cubs game
and the iconic Wrigley Field*

As Team Members we have to:

1. **Check our Identity** – *Look Like We Are On The Team*. When I played sports, one of the aspects I would always look forward to was getting our uniforms. It was something about the uniform. All of us dressed alike and in sync. Ready to battle the opposing team. **We must look like Him**. Once we look like Him, then it is through Him that we will find ourselves equipped to battle the opposition of the world.

2. **Check our Integrity** – *Resemble The Personality Of The Coach/Leader*. Every sport I played, I believed in my coaches. I took on their personalities of achievement and desire to be a winner. We have to act like Christ. In doing so, we take on the mindset of His Characteristics.

Here are two scriptures that validate this:

I. **We have to love one another** (*This shows characteristics of a disciple*). **John 13:35** says *"By this shall all men know that ye are my disciples, if ye have love one to another."* To truly have a sporty spirit, we must love people. We may not always agree or like their acts/behaviors, but we must love them. Jesus loved everyone despite what they did to Him.

Michael sitting behind home plate of the Reds vs Cubs game

II. We must bear fruit. The Bible says in **John 15:8**, *"Herein is my Father glorified, that ye bear much fruit; so shall ye be my disciples."* We must bear much fruit. We can't be team members if we are sitting on our hands doing nothing. If our level of commitment is there, it shows up not just on "game day" (Sunday/Sabbath) but in practice throughout the week as well. It shows in our priorities, how we handle persecution; it shows in our identity, and our integrity.

Walk In Authority Of The Spirit!

Everywhere Jesus went, demons trembled. Without Him saying anything, they recognized Jesus because they recognized His authority. **Luke 4:18** says, *"The Spirit of the Lord is upon me, because he hath anointed me to preach the gospel to the poor; he hath sent me to heal the brokenhearted, to preach deliverance to the captives, and recovering of sight to the blind, to set at liberty them that are bruised."*

*Michael after the Cubs game reflecting
and taking it all in*

Sports has the power to inspire, unite people from diverse backgrounds and create hope. It's so much more than just a game. It can be a tool for transformation.

Countless individuals have felt the life-changing impact of organized sports. Benefits include improved mental and emotional health, confidence, a sense of empowerment, connection, and community.

Dear God: It's game day! Today I place myself in your loving hands. Help me to possess a sporty spirit. I pray that I do not seek individual glory or accolades, but rather that all I do be for your glory, edification, and for the good of your team.
Amen

Chapter 11

HIS TIMING, NOT MINE

"Don't ever exchange God's timing for your deadline."

MH

I was burned out from church as a child and did not want any part of it once I became of age and was out on my own. When I was in college (undergraduate), things were not looking good at all. My grades were failing. Emotionally and spiritually I was disconnected, and physically, I was overweight. I always knew that I wanted to go into the military prior to going off to college, but I wanted to go in as an officer.

As I had embraced my calling to the gospel ministry, I knew that God had more for me to do other than just traditional pastorate ministry. In the book of **Matthew 28:19** the Bible declares, *"Therefore, go and make disciples of all the nations, baptizing them in the name of the Father and the Son and the Holy Ghost."* I felt called to minister in places I'd never been before and to people I'd never seen, without being limited to stain glass windows, steeples, cultures, or denominational barriers. One of my father's former soldiers, who was also a member of our church, asked if I had ever considered the Florida Army National Guard. I had never taken that into consideration, but after hearing the opportunities that joining the guard could present, on April 8, 2009, I joined as a chaplain candidate.

As a chaplain candidate, I was able to learn how to be a soldier while studying under the mentor of a senior chaplain. Also, there were several academic standards that had to be met and obtaining a Master of Divinity (M.Div.) degree was one of them. I started off at South-western Theological Baptist Seminary but returned home as my father was experiencing some difficulty with the pastorate at the time.

Dad and Mom pinning Michael as he became a Chaplain Candidate

My supervisory chaplain, Chaplain Brian Ray advised me that a school called Liberty Baptist Theological Seminary offered courses through distance learning as well as through on-campus intensives at First Baptist Church downtown in Jacksonville, Florida. I took Chaplain Ray's advice and transferred to Liberty Baptist Theological Seminary where I graduated with an M.Div. in Chaplaincy in 2012.

As I studied under Chaplain Ray, the Holy Spirit convicted me that both military and chaplaincy was my calling. Again, I had witnessed how a member of the clergy embraced those he didn't know and who may not have believed what he did. Nevertheless, that did not hinder him from being a ministry of presence and providing pastoral care to God's people. As Chaplain Ray received a promotion and transferred to the Army Reserves, I replaced him at the 927th CSSB (*Combat Support Sustainment Battalion*).

In 2012, I began a new journey within my calling to chaplaincy as I was hired by Community Hospice of Northeast Florida to serve as a staff chaplain. While interviewing for this job, I was asked the question, "What do you know about hospice?" My reply was nothing, but I did know that I knew how to care for people. I am proud to say that I have cared for dying patients and family members for several years now. I have been humble to minister to patients from boarding homes to three-level high rises. From the rural area of the north-side of Jacksonville to the backwoods of Callahan, Florida.

My calling to chaplaincy has not just stopped with hospice. In June of 2014, I graduated from the Jacksonville Sheriff's Office Police Academy as a sworn reserve police officer. Not only did I want to give back to my community through this voluntary service, but I felt called by God to use this as an avenue to minister to those who are in our judicial system. Also, I continue to use the means of my God-given platform in providing a ministry of presence to various professional services and affiliations that I'm involved with.

Although life may appear to be unsteady and yet edifying at the same time, when we cannot see the outcome, we often have the tendency to panic. We look for peace in the midst of the storm, yet peace is not necessarily the absence of problems. Rather, it's the conviction of the outcome. My brothers and sisters, faith is standing in the midst of adversity you see, knowing that there is a greater reality at work. I continuously remind myself that the reality at work is His timing, not mine.

*Michael graduating from the Jacksonville
Sheriff's Office Police Academy. Officer
Christy Conn and my little niece Amoni Jones*

*Michael on Bob Kidd Lake in Prairie Grove,
Arkansas reflecting upon being led beside
the still water*

Dear God: Pull back what I shouldn't be reaching for, take away what doesn't add up, fill in whatever is missing, and pull closer what I've prayed for.

Amen

Chapter 12

You Have No Idea

"When you have been through Hell…
You come out on Fire!"

MH

While deployed (2016-2017), I was sitting down eating lunch one day when a sharp pain shot up my spine. I yelled out loudly in excruciating pain. The medics (1-111th AVN, C - Company) across from me asked, "Chaplain, are you ok?" "No," I replied. "I can't move at all."

They eventually carried me into the ambulance while I was still sitting in the chair. Talk about scary… you have no idea. Upon arriving at the TMC (Troop Medical Center), I was told by the staff that I would possibly not walk again and they needed to send me back to the states for care/re-evaluation was of high consideration. All I heard was *"can't walk again."*

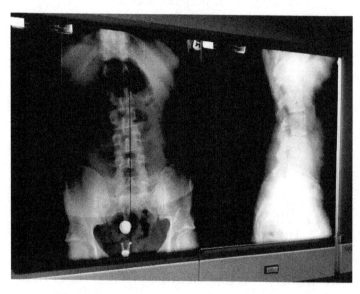

The actual X-Ray of Michael's back

I was horrified and scared. I knew deep down that at this point I was considered combat ineffective. I begged my BC (*Battalion Commander*) to please let me stay. I came up with a way to continue battlefield circulation. I suggested to my BC, "Sir, if you can provide me a gator (Military ATV UTV Side by Side) I can still go to different areas of operations (AOs) and check on soldiers." He agreed!

I was able to get a walker and cane from physical therapy. I continued to preach but I would sit as I did so. I rebuked the words in my spirit that I would not possibly walk again. This did not happen overnight. Approximately two months after the fact, I began to regain strength in my back. Although the pain had begun to subside, I still was not 100%. However, I thank God that I was no longer in the condition that I started in.

I am so grateful for my soldiers who were there for me: SGT Sass and SSG Locke. They waited on me hand and foot. Never complained. It was always, "If you need anything just let me know." They did everything for me but wiped my butt. It's important that you treat others how you would like to be treated. At the end of the day you never know whose hands you will fall into. I am glad that I have always had a strong relationship with soldiers. In my time of need, they did not leave me behind.

Michael inside of the office preparing for the day with his 2nd Chaplain Assistant (Cane)

Upon returning from Iraq 2016-2017, I had the opportunity to train in the Veteran Administrative (VA) System at The South Texas Veterans Healthcare System. I had a wonderful time as a Mental Health Chaplain Fellow. I was able to study with and under great leadership such as Juliana Lesher (current: *National Director of Chaplain Service*), Kerry Haynes (current: *Chief of Chaplain*), and Jim Duke (*ACPE Certified Educator*). My fellow peers: Tray, Hilario, Bob, Andrew, Jon, Todd, and Charles were instrumental in my growth and development. I admire each and every one of those individuals and our group collectively. Upon going to San Antonio, Texas, I had no plan, but I had faith. It was through this faith; however, I had a humbling experience.

Clinical Pastoral Education - Graduation Day Picture: 2018

When I arrived in San Antonio for my Clinical Pastoral Education (CPE) fellowship, I did not know anyone. I had nowhere to stay at the time. I was waiting for an apartment, but the fellowship was starting. I ended up homeless, living out of my Ford Explorer. I would find ways to bathe in order to be prepared for the next day. I was living off of a stipend and I did not have much money. Through creativity and relying on the Lord, I was able to survive. I eventually found a place to live and was able to find used furniture so I had somewhere to lay my head at night.

No one knew this until the end of the 4th unit. As we were in class reflecting one day, I brought this up. I am and will always be grateful for my brothers and sisters who helped me, fed me, and cared for me, in times when they did not have a clue at all what was going on in my life. The genuine spirit to act out of the kindness of their heart brings tears to my eyes even now as I'm writing, looking, and reflecting upon these very words.

Clinical Pastoral Education (CPE) South Texas - 2018

Nevertheless, the Lord brought into my life someone by the name of V. V, as I refer to her, has always been an encourager and supporter. I find comfort in being able to be myself around her, even though she can get on my nerves at times (LOL). I can recall when she attempted to bring me happiness by taking me to a restaurant. As she thought this would be a good idea, my stubbornness got in the way, and I soon became resistant. I did not want to go at all, as I can be picky. As we were riding down the road in a heated dialogue, her daughter, "Toni the Tiger" belted out "relax!" We could not help but laugh and reflect upon how petty we were acting and how it took a child to inspire grown adults to see how we were not setting a good example.

You see, when life is up and down, there is a voice telling us to "relax." When it seems hopeless and you're homeless, "relax." When you feel like giving up, "relax." It has been said that *"Family and friendships are two of the greatest facilitators of happiness."* –**John C. Maxwell**.

My brothers and sisters, when your normal has been disrupted, *reacting doesn't outweigh responding*. The way we respond to confusion and discomfort is in the relaxation of knowing there is a God that is able to heal a broken heart and mend broken relationships. We are not made to do life alone. It doesn't matter how strong, educated, talented, gifted, anointed, or connected you are. We need community and connectedness in order to be successful in this area. Sometimes we have to be quarantined in order to appreciate the small things about life.

The time had come after CPE graduation to finally get a job. As there were several options, Fayetteville, Arkansas presented itself. In all honesty, I thought I was going to Fayetteville, North Carolina. It was my intention to join the Army Reserves and find a unit at Fort Bragg, North Carolina. Nevertheless, coming to Arkansas has been a great experience. It reminds me of undergraduate school in Harrogate, Tennessee. I have been able to meet several people. If I tried to name them all I would forget, so in respect I will not attempt to. However, they have helped me, supported me, prayed for me; they've prayed with, laughed, and cried with me. WOO PIG!

Listen, I am blessed to be a Clinical Chaplain and CPE Supervisor. I am blessed to be a son, brother, uncle, cousin, soldier and Veteran. I am blessed to be a friend and mentor.

I'm also blessed to be the Michael God has made me. I make a living off the very things that used to eat me up privately. Now, I am able to enter into the sacred space of others,

When life throws you a rod then you should start fishing

free from judgment and bitterness, facilitating spiritual healing by which he/she experiences the Divine and what brings meaning and purpose to their lives.

There are a lot of people who are caught up in going viral, but I am into making history! There's only so much that you can sweep under the rug until it's time to vacuum. The book has allowed me to plug into the power derived from my painful experiences in my life. I am humbled by the fact you have taken your time to support me and the message the Lord has given me. It is my prayer that the book inspires you to be yourself, whatever that looks like, and for you to be comfortable in that space. More importantly, allow it to inspire you to be **MORE HUMBLE**.

Dear Lord: Cover the vulnerable, protect the fragile, embrace the rejected, comfort the inconsolable, calm those who are anxious, and energize the apathetic.

Amen

Obedience Releases Opportunity

ACKNOWLEDGEMENTS

I thank God for providing His hand of grace to be upon me in the midst of my foolishness. To my parents Patricia A. Robinson and Morris J. Halyard, thank you for your parenthood. To my siblings, family, friends: to include but not limited to *T-Moe, Capt., Pooh*, R.I.P Sam Felton, Jemelle, Big Earnest, "D" and church family at United Missionary Baptist Church (UMBC). Thank you.

I also want to humbly acknowledge the painful relationships and those who left me when I was at a point where I thought I needed them the most. It has been through those experiences where I've learned that things can move from impossible to inevitable.

CLOSING THOUGHTS

In my young life thus far, what have I learned? I believe that it's about the journey. Through the journey, you are exposed to the blessed results. Nevertheless, this cycle is all inclusive in which it never ends until you are dead.

Identity is a funny character. Just when you think you have defined yourself or that life has defined you, my brothers and sisters, there's always another chapter or challenge. This is the humbling experience or theory that is put forward as a premise to be maintained or proved. For me, it has enabled me to get out of my comfort zone. And until you do, you may never know the magnitude of what you are capable of.

Until my death, *"May the words of my mouth and the meditation of my heart be pleasing in your sight, O Lord, my strength, and my Redeemer."*

Psalm 19:14

About the Author

"The problem with "being strong" is that nobody expects you to ever have a weak moment."

In this book, I share how I have come to find meaning and purpose through my flaws and faith. My journey to being "More Humble" has allowed me to play to my strengths and train to my weaknesses. In the midst of being "A preacher's kid," chaplain, and spiritual leader of humanity, it is my prayer that my brokenness helps you more than my "put-togetherness" ever did.

Holding a Bachelor of Arts (Lincoln Memorial University), Master of Divinity (Liberty School of Divinity), Michael J. Halyard is a Board-Certified (BCC) Clinical Pastoral Education (CPE) Certified Educator and United States Army (MAJ) Combat Veteran. With

13 units of CPE, Department of Psychology: Moralities of Everyday Life (Certificate) -Yale University and continuing academia Doctor of Ministry (D.Min.) at Erskine Theological Seminary.

My theological training has been accomplished with the knowledge and conviction that God has "called" me to ministry as a servant of His Kingdom in a variety of settings. As I serve men and women within congregations, communities, clinical and military settings, I'm compelled by the Holy Spirit by acting as an advocate of spiritual, moral, ethical maturity and resiliency, in order to assist God's people, their families, and other authorized personnel in embracing the Divine, while providing a ministry of presence.

Please connect on these social media platforms:

Facebook: Michael Halyard

Instagram: Halyardbows

Twitter: Halyard Ministries @MichaelHalyard

LinkedIn: Michael J. Halyard

Made in the USA
Middletown, DE
23 July 2020

13498842R00070